Disney's Bambi 2

D0904569

Phidal

© Disney Enterprises, Inc.
2006 Produced and Published by Phidal Publishing Inc.
All rights reserved.
www.phidal.com

Plenty of Paws!

Match the animals with their paw prints.

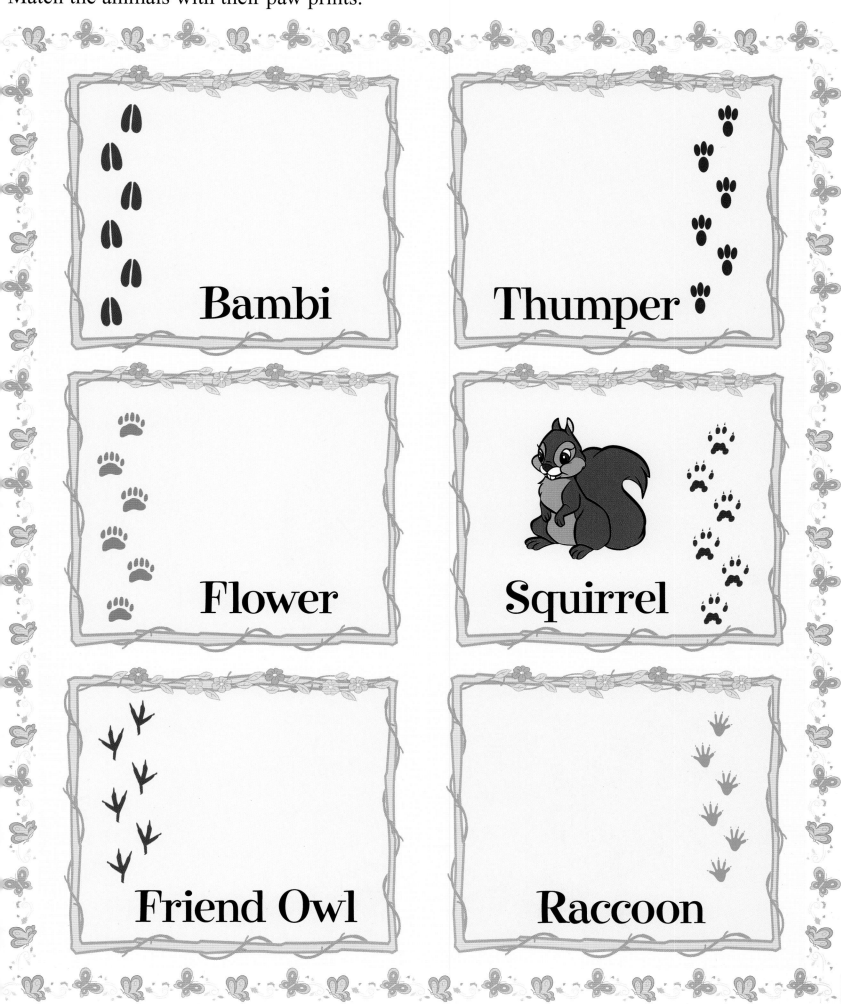

Bambi

Thumper

Flower

Squirrel

Friend Owl

Raccoon

Palette Match

Place each plant or animal in its matching square with your stickers.

Elders and Youngsters

Use your stickers to help the parents find their children at the end of a fun-filled day.

The Friendly Forest

Use your stickers to decorate the scene.

Meet the Characters

Answer these questions with the help of your stickers.

Who is Bambi
in love with?

Who is
Bambi's father?

Who hops and
has long ears?

Who is green and
lives in a pond?

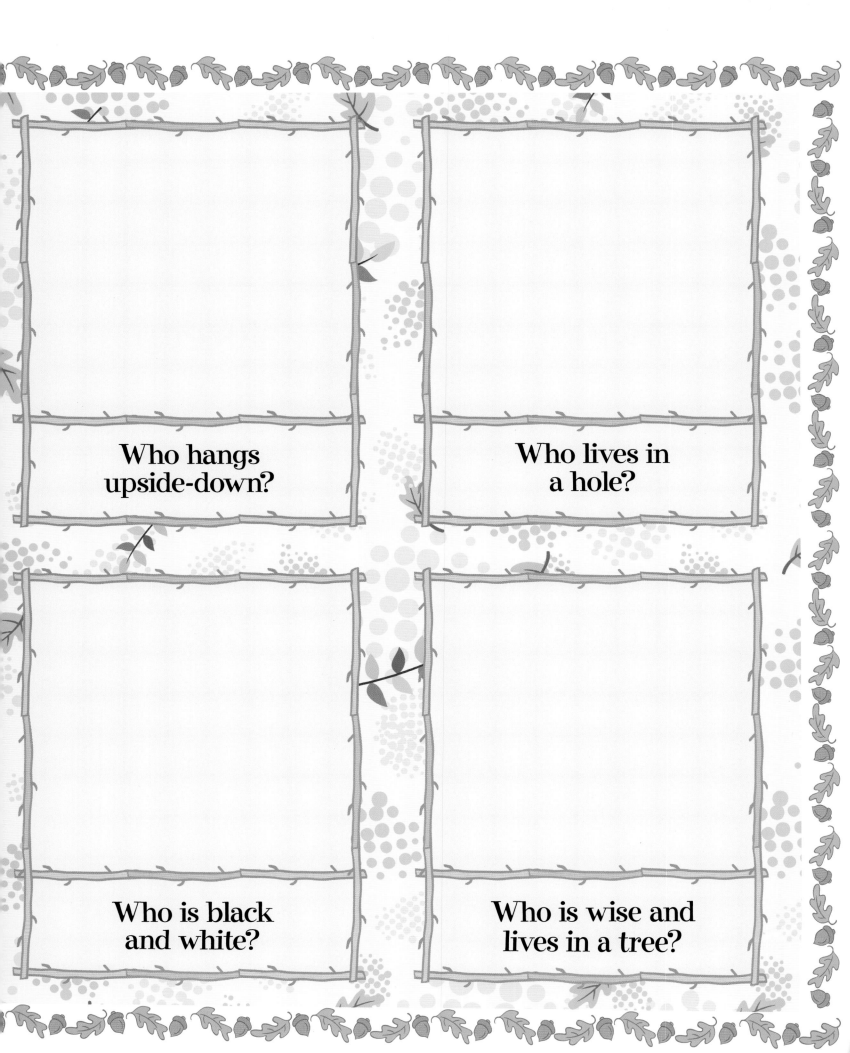

Who hangs
upside-down?

Who lives in
a hole?

Who is black
and white?

Who is wise and
lives in a tree?

13

Matching Opposites

Use your stickers to match each opposite.

Awake

Asleep

Front

Back

Big

Small

Standing

Sitting

Left

Right

One

Many

What Is Missing?

Look closely at the first image. Now complete the scene below with your stickers.

Disney's
BROTHER
BEAR

Phidal

© Disney Enterprises, Inc.
2006 Produced and Published by Phidal Publishing Inc.
All rights reserved.
www.phidal.com

Who's Who?

Use your stickers to identify each character.

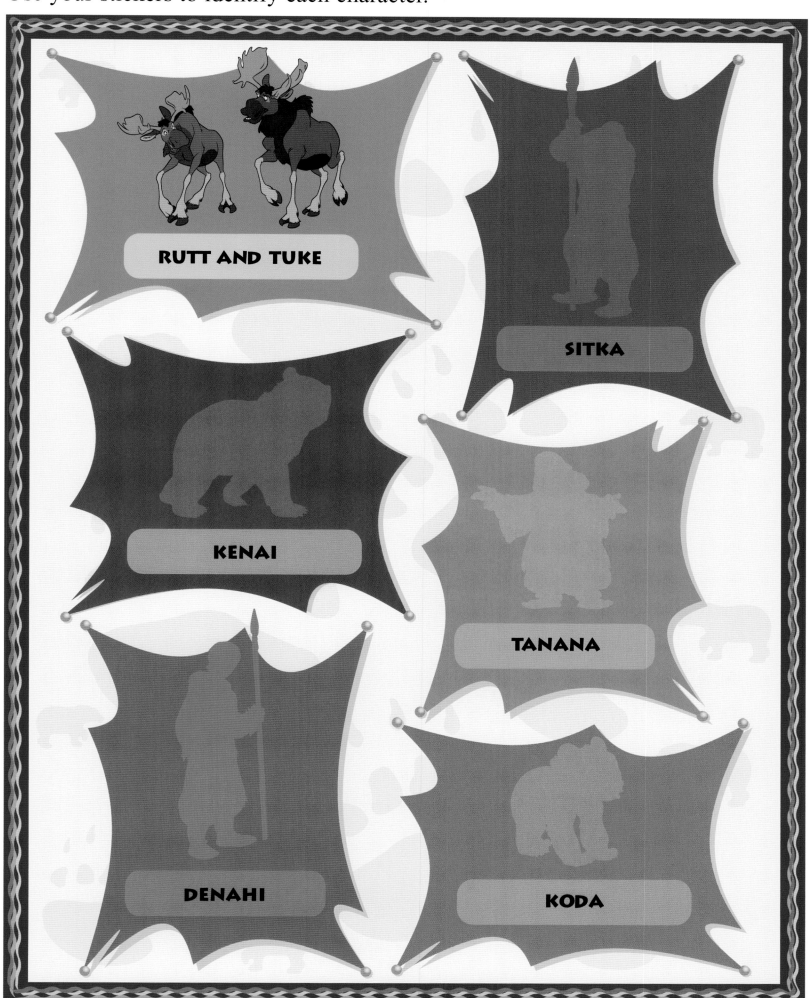

RUTT AND TUKE

SITKA

KENAI

TANANA

DENAHI

KODA

Big Bear, Little Bear

Use your stickers to find each opposite.

OLD

YOUNG

BRAVE

AFRAID

PAW UP

PAW DOWN

FAST

SLOW

HAPPY

SAD

ASLEEP

AWAKE

BIG

SMALL

STANDING

SITTING

FRONT

OPEN

CLOSED

BACK

Friends in the Forest

Use your stickers to decorate the scene.

What Comes Next?

Place your stickers in the correct order to complete the sequence.

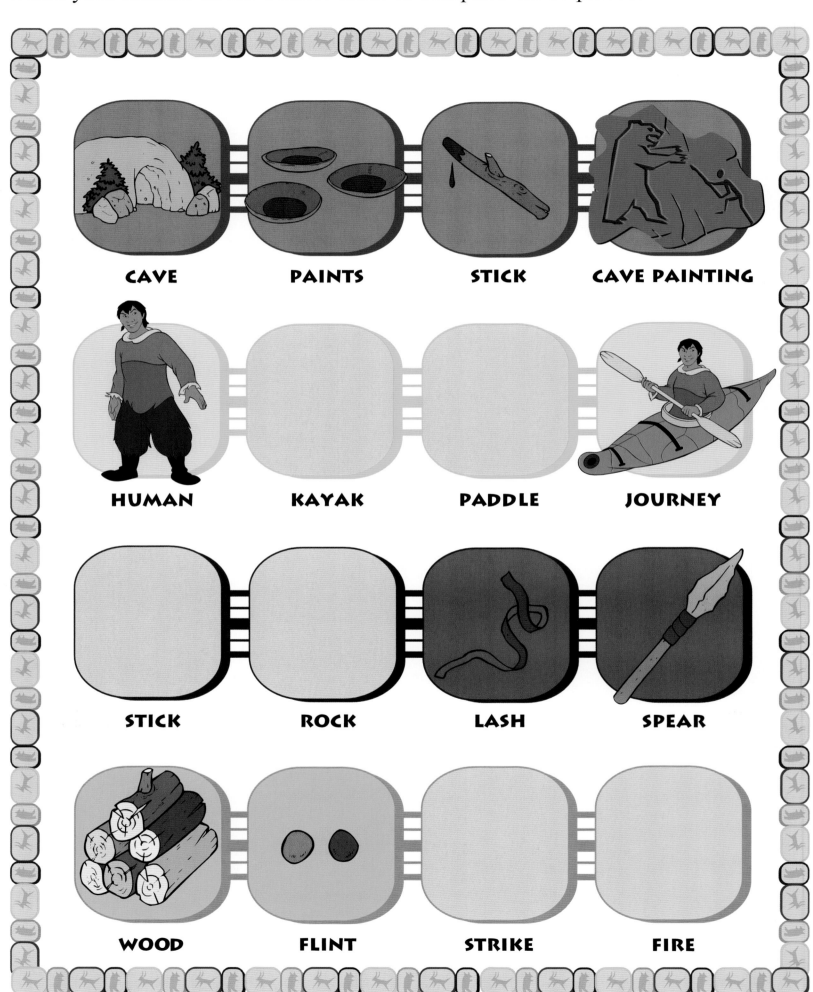

CAVE   PAINTS   STICK   CAVE PAINTING

HUMAN   KAYAK   PADDLE   JOURNEY

STICK   ROCK   LASH   SPEAR

WOOD   FLINT   STRIKE   FIRE

Big and Small

Place your stickers in order from smallest to largest.

ANIMALS

HUMANS

THINGS

Matching Totems

Match each brother with his totem and the animal it represents.

BROTHER	TOTEM	ANIMAL

Follow the Trails

Use your stickers to help these companions find each other.

Who Am I?

Use your stickers to match each animal with its description.

I have curved horns on my head.

I carry my house on my back.

I swim and leap in the water.

I have a black mask and a ringed tail.

I have prickly quills along my back.

My tail is as long as my small body.

Disney's chicken little

Phidal

© Disney Enterprises, Inc.
2006 Produced and Published by Phidal Publishing Inc.
All rights reserved.
www.phidal.com

Friends and Family

Use your stickers to correctly identify each character.

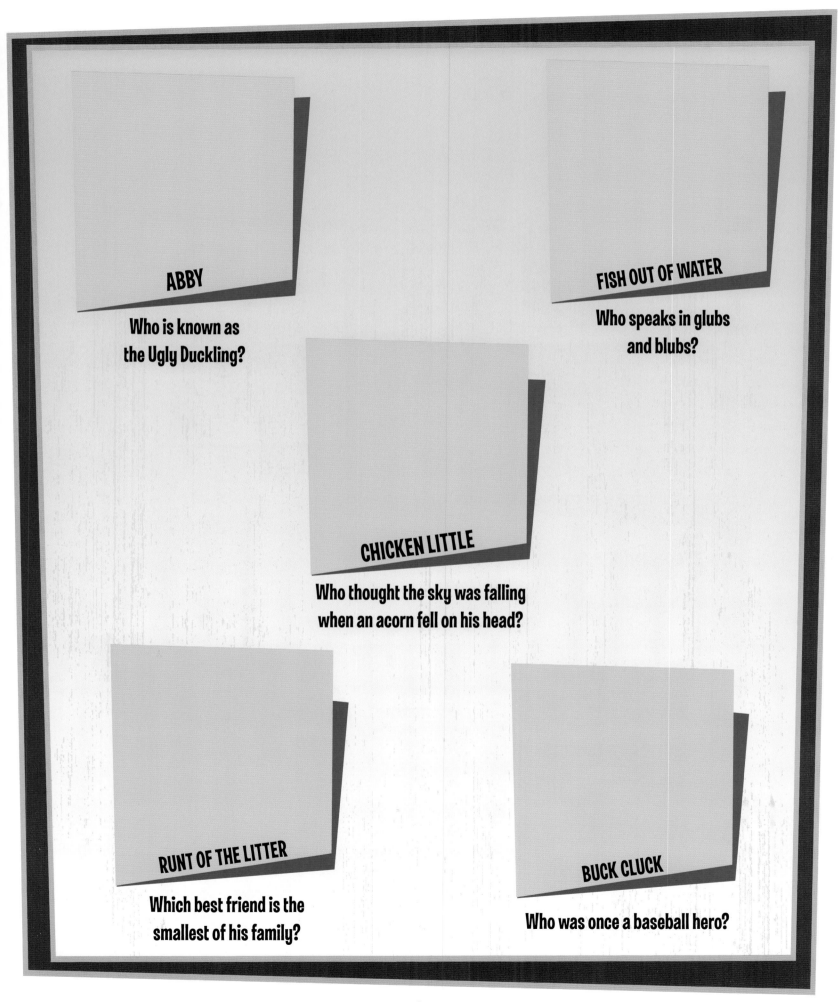

ABBY

Who is known as
the Ugly Duckling?

FISH OUT OF WATER

Who speaks in glubs
and blubs?

CHICKEN LITTLE

Who thought the sky was falling
when an acorn fell on his head?

RUNT OF THE LITTER

Which best friend is the
smallest of his family?

BUCK CLUCK

Who was once a baseball hero?

Custom Cars

Use your stickers to match each quirky car with its owner.

Between Classes

Use your stickers to make the bottom scene look like the top.

Main Street

Use your stickers to complete this bustling scene.

Big Chicken, Little Chicken
Use your stickers to match the characters to their opposites.

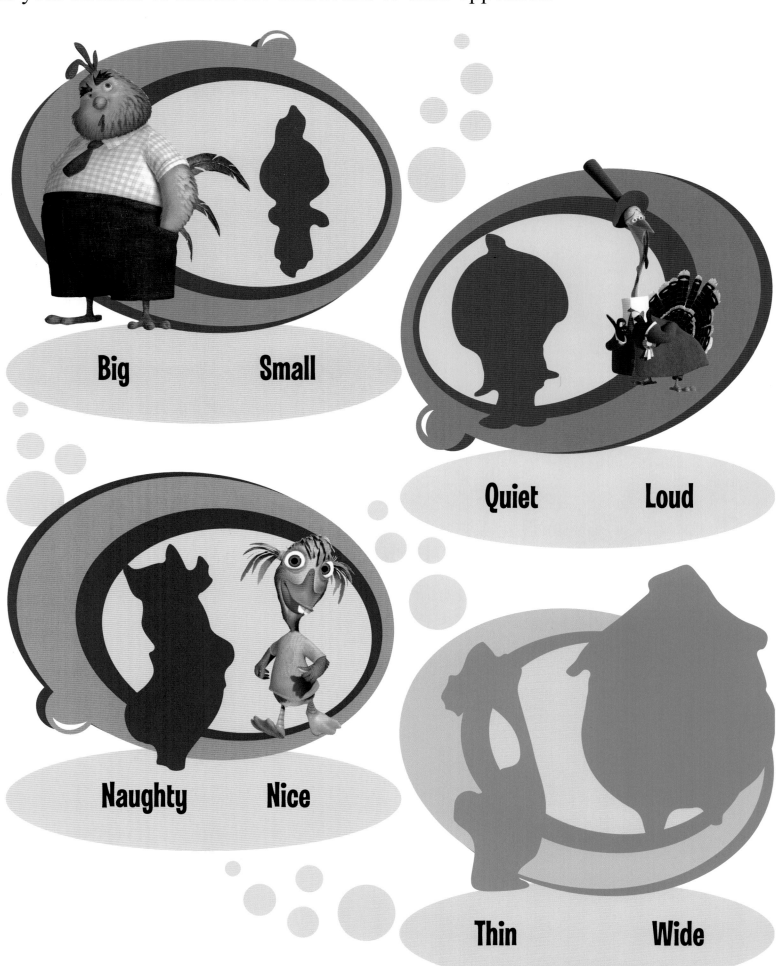

Big   **Small**

Quiet   **Loud**

Naughty   **Nice**

Thin   **Wide**

12

All Around Oakey Oaks

Use your stickers to match the characters to the places where they belong.

Perfect Pairs

Use your stickers to match these items with their owners.

Who Goes There?
Use your stickers to identify each character's footprint.

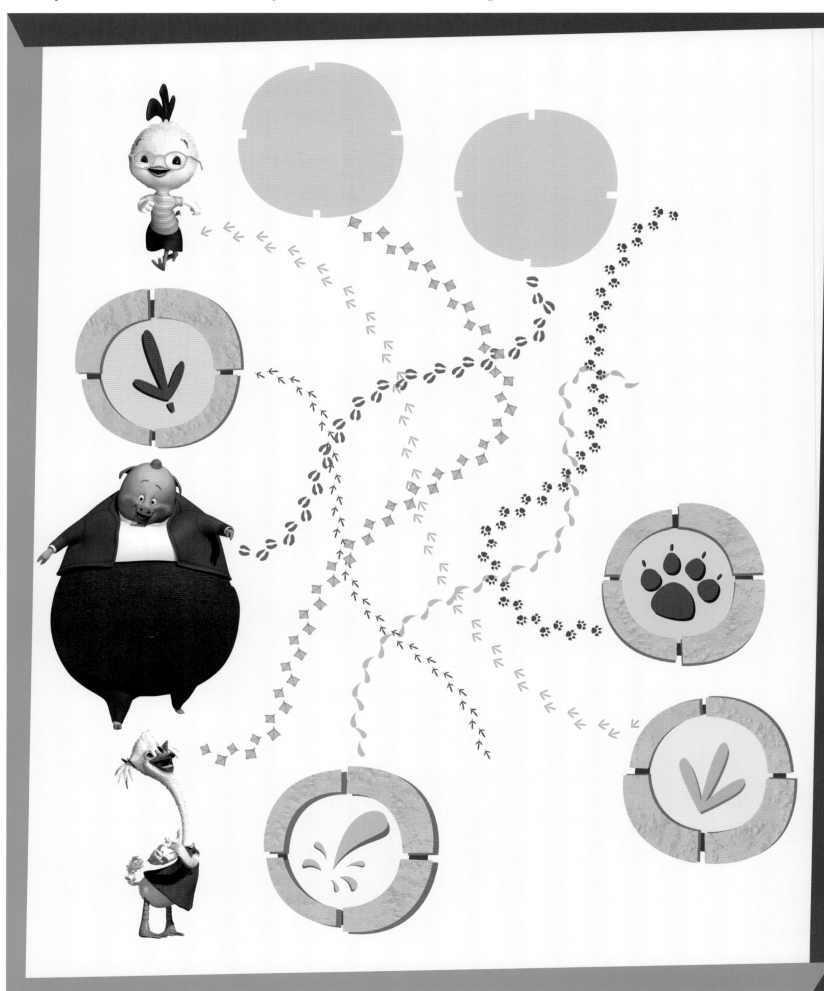

Phidal

© Disney Enterprises, Inc.
2006 Produced and Published by Phidal Publishing Inc.
All rights reserved.
www.phidal.com

Who Am I?

Answer these questions with the help of your stickers.

Who won the Golden Udder Award?

Who can yodel?

Who owns Patch of Heaven?

Who wears a purple hat?

Who wants to be a hero?

Who doesn't have an ear for music?

Count From 1 to 10

Finish each series to get the right number.

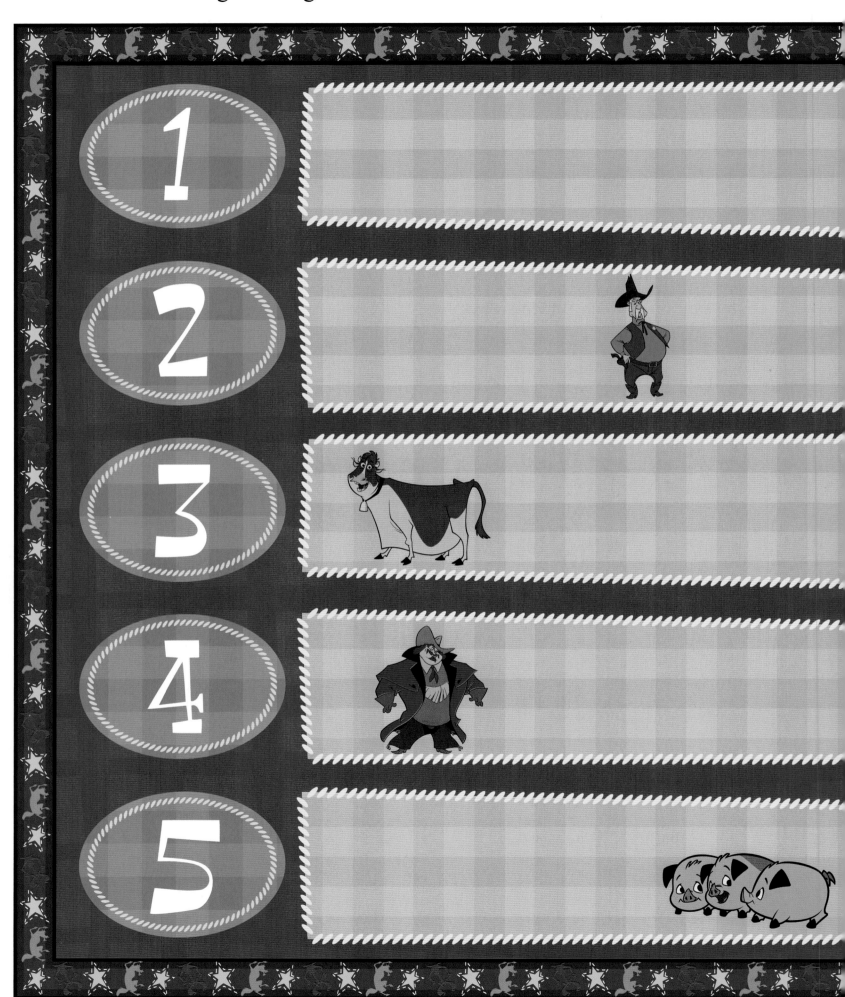

A Patch of Heaven

Use your stickers to decorate the scene.

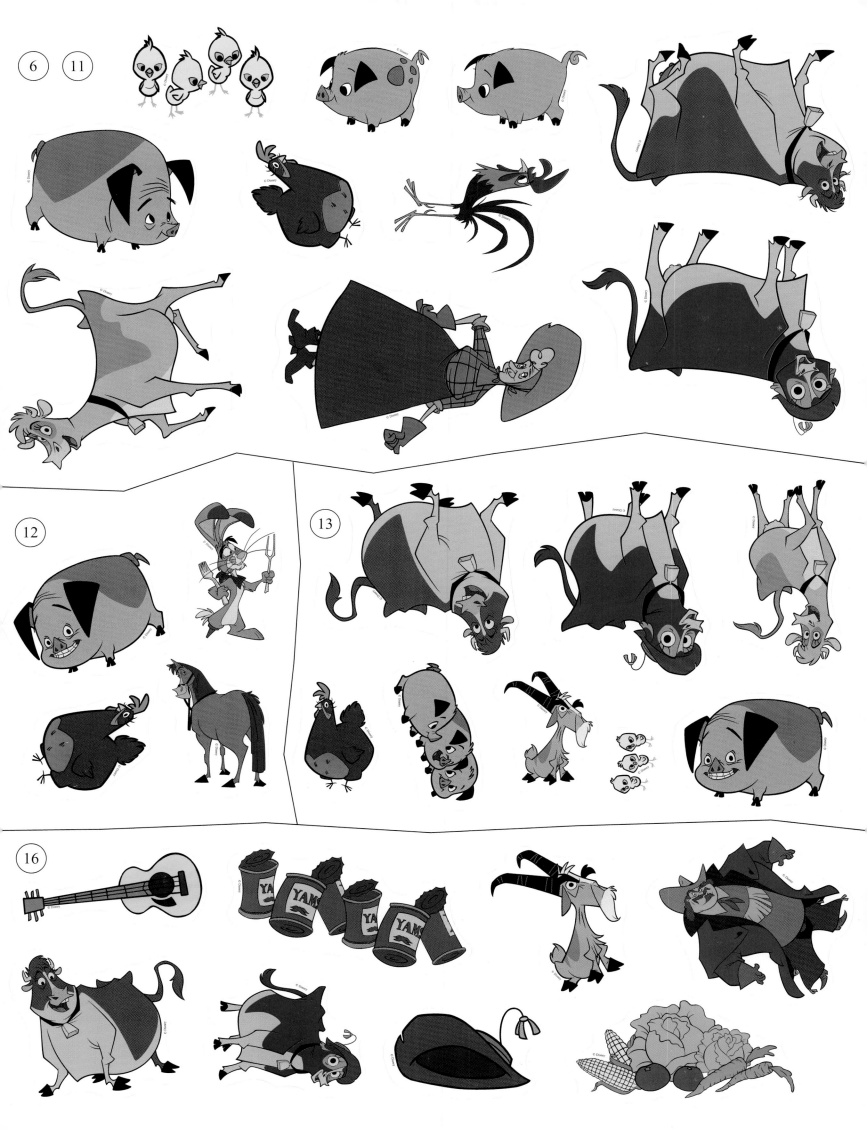

Prairie Shades

Place the missing animals next to their matching palette.

What Is Missing?

Look closely at the first image. Now complete the scene below with your stickers.

Barnyard Party

Place the stickers over their matching shadows.

Pair Them Up
Match each character with the missing food or object.

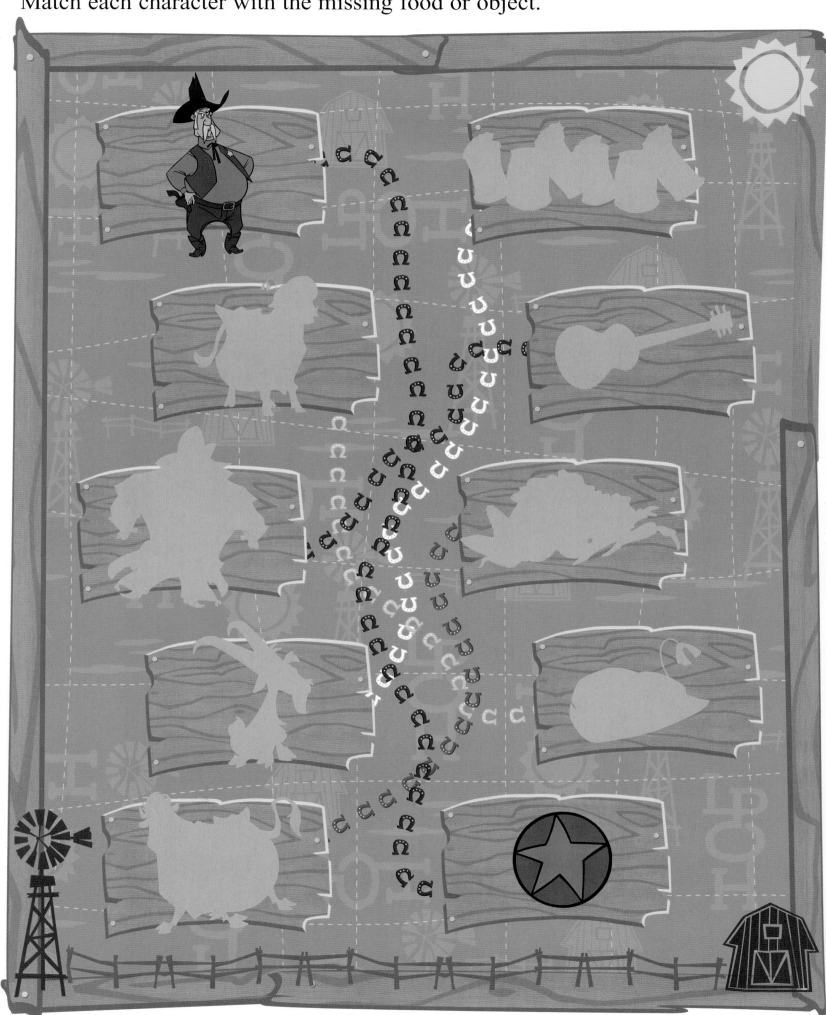

DISNEY'S
THE
LION KING 1½

P Phidal

© Disney Enterprises, Inc.
2006 Produced and Published by Phidal Publishing Inc.
All rights reserved.
www.phidal.com

Meet the Characters

Place your stickers in the right box.

Timon

Pumbaa

Uncle Max

Timon's Mother

Simba

Rafiki

Time to Add and Subtract
Use your stickers to solve the problems below.

The Oasis

Use your stickers to complete the scene.

6

14

15

16

Matching Opposites

Use your stickers to match each opposite.

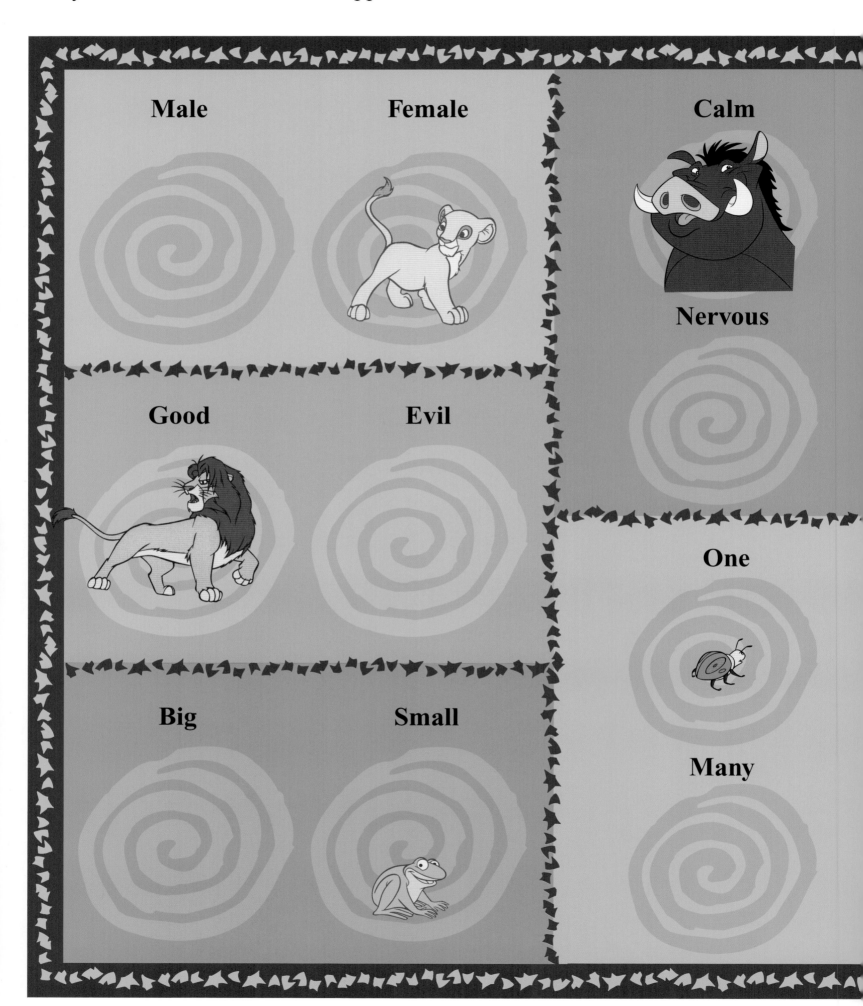

Male   Female   Calm

Nervous

Good   Evil

One

Big   Small

Many

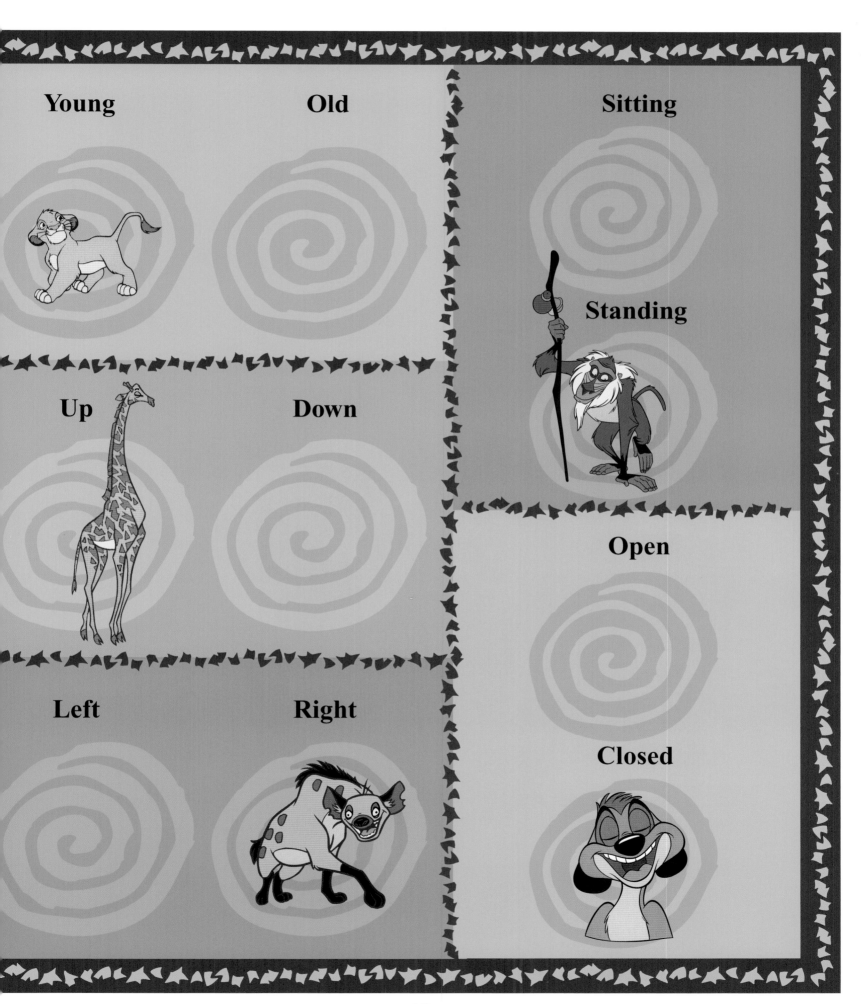

Young   **Old**   **Sitting**

Standing

Up   **Down**

Open

Left   **Right**

Closed

Matching Palette

Place each character next to the matching combination.

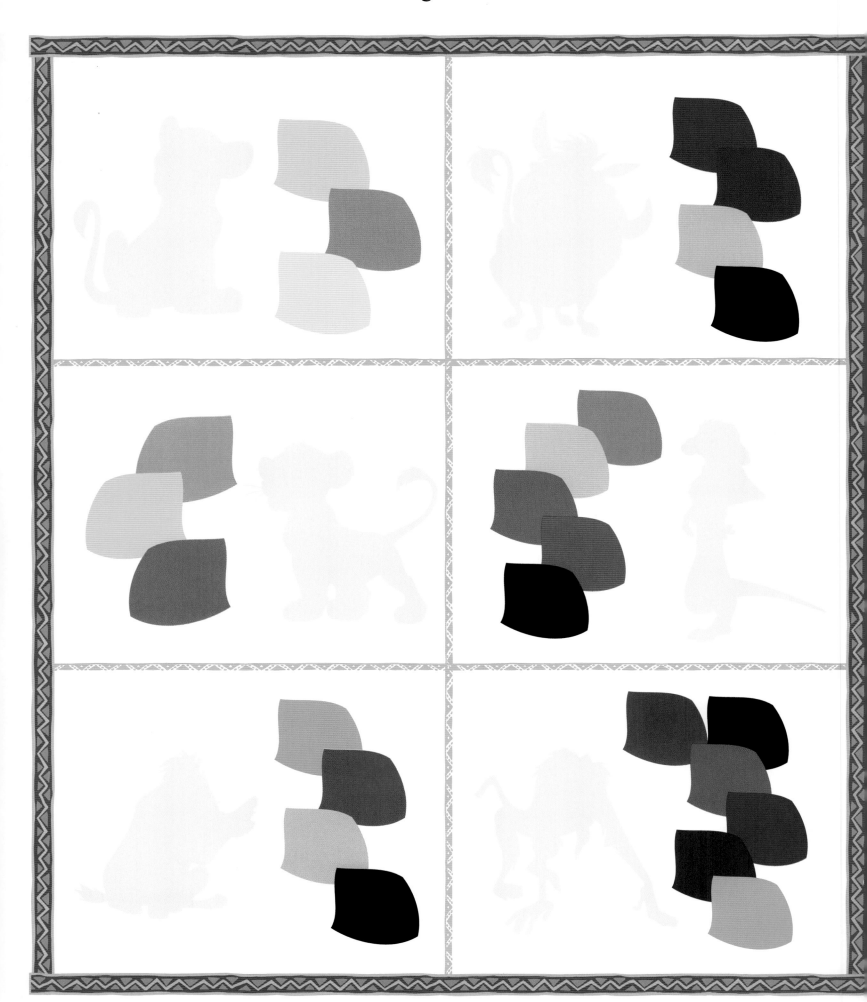

Where Do They Belong?

Which animals can you find in each of these settings?

Pride Rock

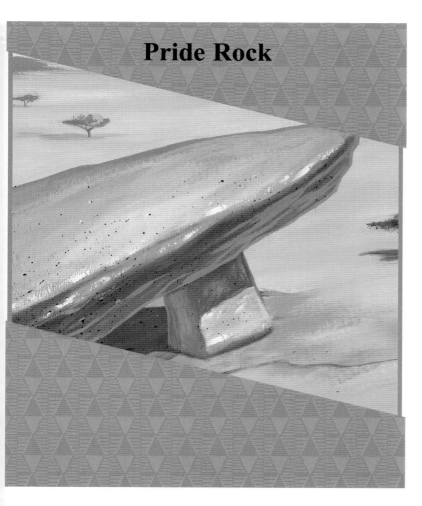

Elephant Graveyard

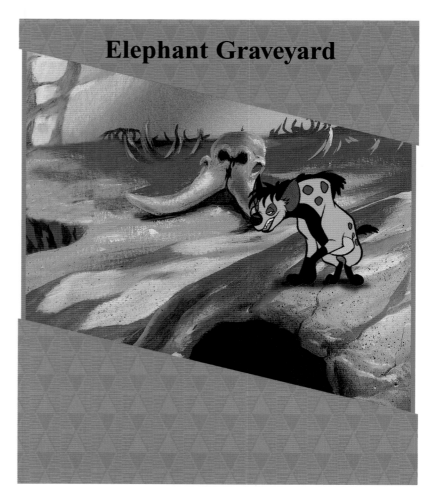

Meerkat Village

The Oasis

Complete the Scene

Place your stickers over the shadows to complete the scene.

Phidal

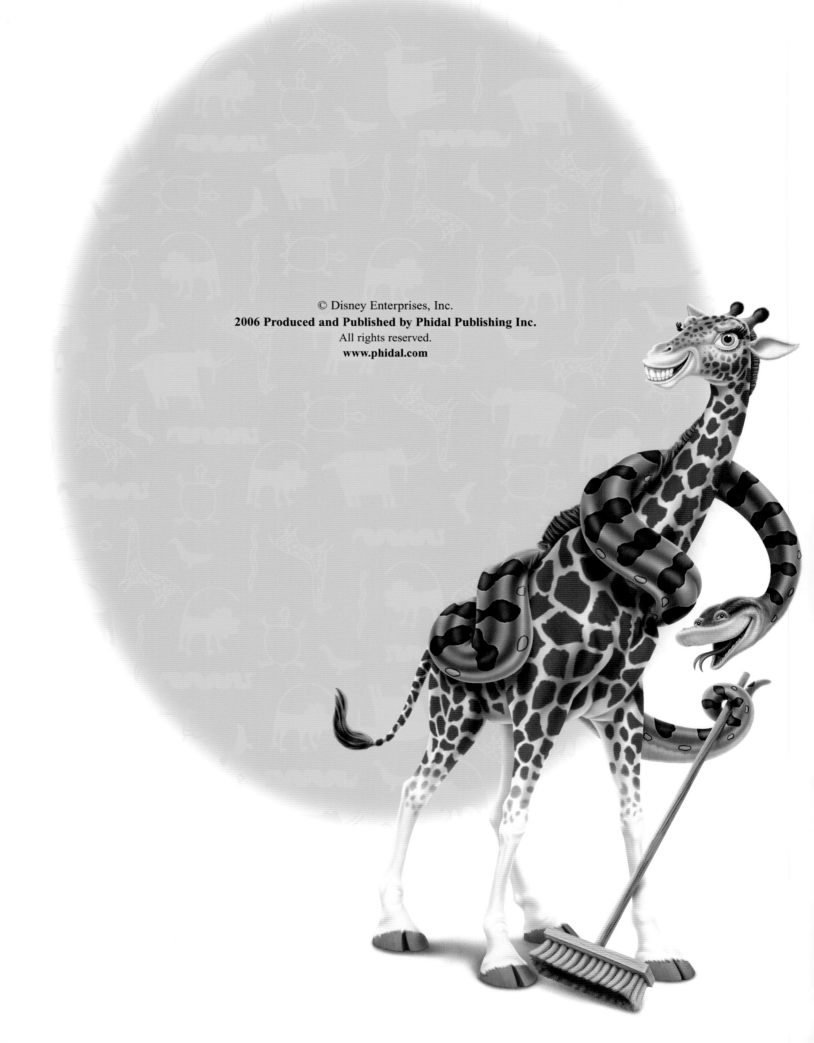

© Disney Enterprises, Inc.
2006 Produced and Published by Phidal Publishing Inc.
All rights reserved.
www.phidal.com

Meet the Characters

Use your stickers to identify each animal.

Samson

Ryan

Nigel

Bridget

Larry

Benny

Match the Pattern
Use your stickers to match each animal to its pattern.

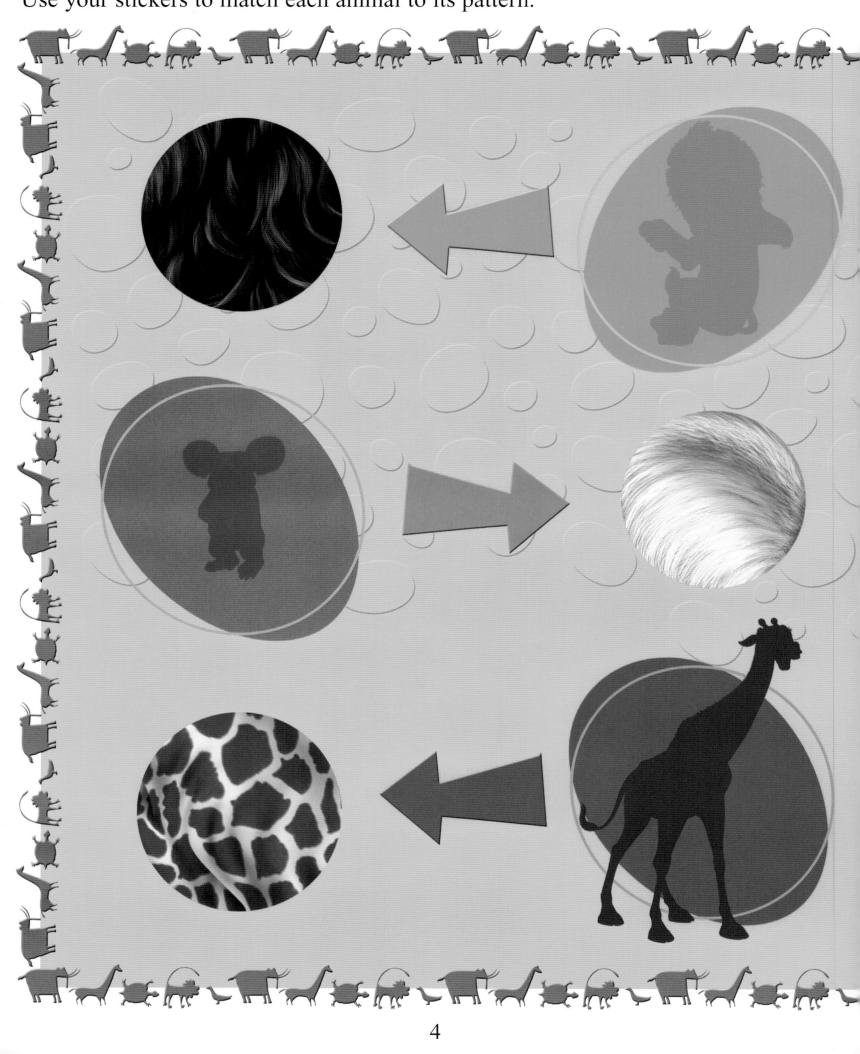

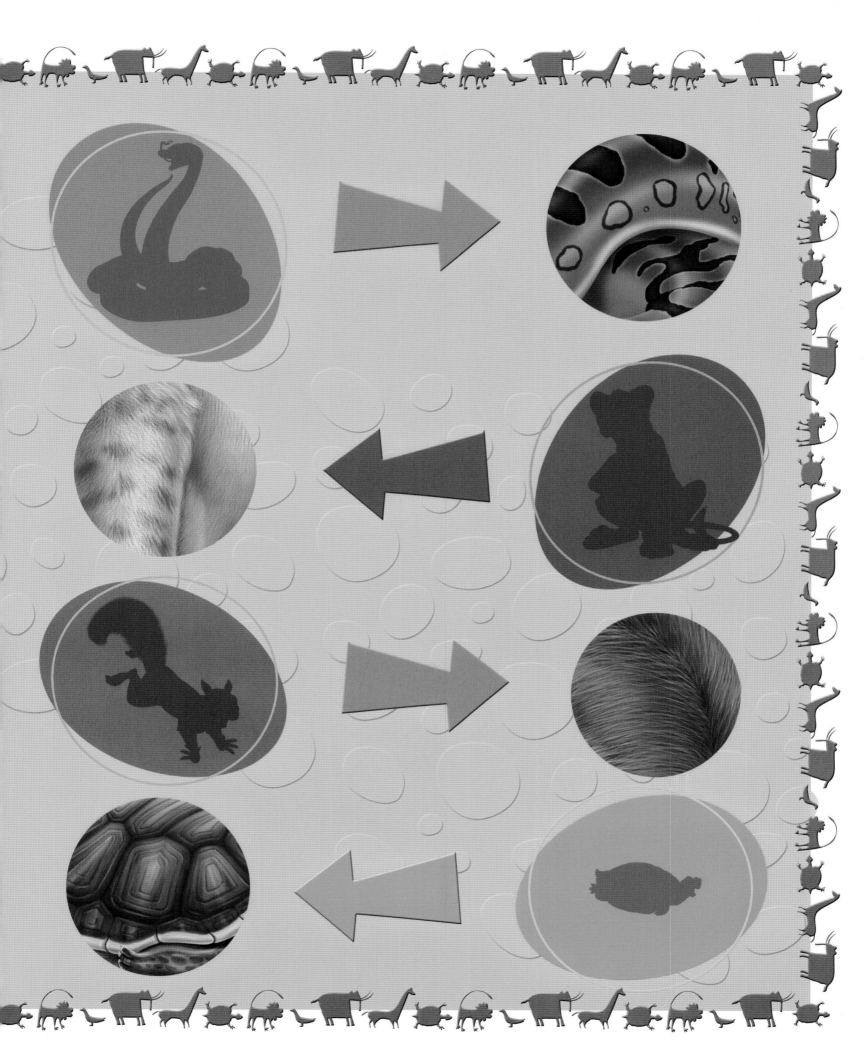

The Zoo at Night

Use your stickers to decorate the scene.

Time to Add and Subtract
Use your stickers to solve each problem.

Assembly in the Cavern

Place your stickers on the shadows to complete this scene.